Then & Now

SEVENOAKS

SEVENOAKS

Then & Now
SEVENOAKS

COMPILED BY PHILLIP BURGESS

TEMPUS

First published 2001
Copyright © Phillip Burgess, 2001

Tempus Publishing Limited
The Mill, Brimscombe Port,
Stroud, Gloucestershire, GL5 2QG

ISBN 0 7524 2200 6

Typesetting and origination by
Tempus Publishing Limited
Printed in Great Britain by
Midway Colour Print, Wiltshire

The school gymnasium of Sevenoaks School was built in 1890, and also doubled as an assembly hall. The old photograph shows pupils using the gym apparatus, around 1908. The gymnasium used to stand to the right of the School House when looking at it from the Upper High Street. While it is clear that the physical exercise aspect of education was important, even in the nineteenth century, the school governors of the day would be impressed to see the wide spectrum of sport and leisure activities available to the Sevenoaks School pupil of today. The school has cricket pitches, indoor and out, rugby pitches, an athletics track, modern gymnasium, and two squash courts. Cross country running takes place in Knole Park, and the local reservoir is used for sailing. Other sports include netball, hockey and rounders.

CONTENTS

Turret in Knole.

ACKNOWLEDGEMENTS

Thanks must also go the following people: Dawn Foster; Andrew Lister, Sevenoaks Reference Library; Ian Streeter; Arthur Hills and the West Kent District Association Branch of the Cyclists Touring Club; Andy Seall, Sevenoaks Town Band; Mr E. Diplock and Sevenoaks Town Football Club; Mr R.F. Williams, Sevenoaks Bowling Club; Mr and Mrs D. Knutton, First Sevenoaks Scout Group; Mr and Mrs Bird; Revd Pat Hopkins, St Bartholomew's church; Mr & Mrs A. Sturdy; Eric Keys, The Sevenoaks Society (for use of the Gordon Anckorn collection); Sub Officer Hogben, Leading Firefighter Barrett and Firefighters Miles, Winchcombe and Dempsey from Sevenoaks Fire Brigade; Mr T.R. Cookson, Headmaster, and Brian Raynor, archivist, Sevenoaks School; Mr C. Gough; Nick Lynch and Mr T. Schofield, Ide Hill Cricket Club; Fifth Year class pupils and their teacher, Sevenoaks School.

I would like to express my sincere thanks to Steven Streeter, who made this book possible by taking the contemporary photographs. Once again he has done an excellent job and made the hard work involved fun and interesting. Our searches for this book took us up towers, down valleys, through mud and all during the best winter weather that could be thrown at us.

INTRODUCTION

Sevenoaks began life as a market town in Saxon times, and its name is derived from the Saxon word for seven oaks, *Seouenaca*. Sevenoaks is so-called because, as its name implies, there were seven oak trees in the town. The original seven oaks were said to date from around AD 950, and would have been at the heart of the original settlement, possibly near where St Nicholas' church stands today. The original trees were probably felled by the Normans. However, as the town's motto is *Floreant Septum Quercus*, meaning 'May the Seven Oaks Flourish', the seven oaks have been replanted many times over the years. Their location has changed, from the centre of town to the Vine Cricket Ground and to London Road, but the oaks remain an important part of the town. Historically, Sevenoaks was part of the Great Manor of Otford, which was held by the Archbishops of Canterbury. However, economic development in the town at the beginning of the thirteenth century, with the establishment of a market, meant that Sevenoaks became a manor in its own right. Economic success came quickly to the town. This was mainly due to its excellent location, as it was conveniently situated halfway between London and the south coast. Sevenoaks could serve the two major routes in operation at the time, the road to London and the road to Dartford. The area in and around the town boasted a large number of landed estates. This also helped the economic empowerment of the town. Such estates included Bradbourne, Chevening Kippington, Knole, Montreal and Wildernesse. Another sign of the success of the town was the number of public houses. By 1389, sixty-three houses were in the brewing business.

More recent developments have come about since the arrival of the railway. Sevenoaks has two stations, one known as the Bat and Ball, the other as Sevenoaks, although it was originally called Tub's Hill after that area of the town. The first line into the town was opened in 2 June 1862, when the East Kent Railway was linked to the Sevenoaks Railway, along the Darent Valley. On 30 June 1862, the South Eastern Railway Company won Parliamentary approval to build a direct line to Sevenoaks from London via Orpington. The directors of the Sevenoaks Railway protested at the decision but it was overruled. The new line meant that much heavy construction work was required, and an influx of labour was necessary. A tunnel had to be excavated for the new line, and during this work, an underground stream was tapped, flooding the work. A pump was installed to solve the problem, and from this the Oak Lane reservoir was formed, becoming the main water supply for the town. The line was finally opened on 2 March 1868, offering direct access to Charing Cross and Cannon Street.

The arrival of the railway meant that business could be carried out further from home, and so the growth of Sevenoaks as a commuter town began in earnest. Before the railway, a trip to London was arduous, and so a day trip was out of the question. However, with the railway, it was possible to live in Sevenoaks but work in London. The town's development was further accelerated by the electrification of the railway in 1934.

The rise of Sevenoaks as a market town and more predominately as a commuter town can be seen from the population increase. In 1801 there were 2,279 inhabitants, and soon before the railway came there were 5,061 in 1841. By 1951 this had shot up to 14,834 and ten years later stood at 17,604. The population today stands at just over 18,500.

The increased population put a strain on the town and so many new residential estates were developed. At the time of writing, the latest development in Riverhead had only taken place in the last few years. The town has spread outwards from the hub along the High Street and London Road, and now comprises of an area of some fifteen and a half square kilometres.

Sevenoaks and surrounding villages have played host to many famous names throughout history. Visits by royalty have been numerous. Kings Edward I, Henry VII and Henry VIII were visitors to Otford and Knole. In more recent times, Jane Austen stayed in the town at the Red House in the High Street. At the time it was owned by Dr Francis Austen, Jane's great uncle. She also spent time at nearby Chevening. Jane Austen wasn't the only author to come to the town. H.G. Wells lived at 23 Eardley Road, during 1894. It was here that he finished writing the first ever science fiction thriller, *The Time Machine*.

Charles Essinhigh-Corke an artist and photographer was a famous resident. For many years, he had studios in the town, although he was best known for his many watercolours of Knole. He produced many popular pictures of Sevenoaks, and during World War One, took many photographs of soldiers on their way to battle. He died in 1922. Vita Sackville-West grew up at Knole, and she is best remembered for her book on the House (*Knole and the Sackvilles*) and for the gardens she created at Sissinghurst Castle.

The nearby village of Westerham was overshadowed by the residency of one person in particular, Winston Churchill. In 1922 he bought the property of Chartwell. During this time it was used mainly as a weekend home. However, this all changed when the Conservatives were defeated in May 1930, and the house was shut up for a time. Now in the hands of the National Trust, Chartwell serves as a fitting tribute to its most famous owner.

As can be seen from this brief history, the town has a lot to offer the visitor. It is rich in history and architecture. It has stately homes, ancient churches, parks and gardens. There are also numerous recreational facilities on offer, from cinema to the theatre to sports. There are many old pubs, restaurants and hotels, and improved shopping facilities with the recent opening of a shopping centre in what was Bligh's car park.

Most of the old photographs in this book are from postcards I have in my collection, or which have been kindly lent to me. Most date from the late nineteenth to the early twentieth centuries. Every effort has been made to obtain copyright permission where necessary. As is usual when delving into the history of a subject, some dates have been incorrectly noted or mistaken over the years. I have tried as far as possible to corroborate any discrepancies with other sources. I apologise if I have mis-spelt a name or incorrectly noted a date or fact.

BIBLIOGRAPHY

Sevenoaks Recollections – Edwin Thompson
A Sevenoaks Camera – Gordon Anckorn
Sevenoaks Memories – Gordon Anckorn
Sevenoaks Past – Christopher Rayner
100 years growth in Sevenoaks – Sevenoaks Society History Section
Sevenoaks Chronicle of the Century – Bob Ogley and Roger Perkins
The pleasant town of Sevenoaks – A History – Sir John Dunlop
Victorian Churches of Kent - Roger Homan
West Kent and the Weald – John Newman
Knole and the Sackvilles – Vita Sackville-West

This is a photograph of the Cartoon Gallery in the stately house of Knole, the family home of Lord Sackville. Knole has three long galleries, each with an adjoining state bedroom. One of the largest private houses in the country, Knole has thirteen state rooms which are open to the public. The Cartoon Gallery is so named after a set of six copies of Raphael's cartoons produced by Daniel Mytens. These were presented by Charles I to Lionel Cranfield, First Earl of Middlesex, and brought to Knole by his daughter, Frances, who married the Fifth Earl of Dorset. Knole boasts many riches, including some unique Jacobean furniture, tapestries, silver and paintings by Van Dyck, Kneller, Lely, Hoppner, Wootton and Gainsborough. Many items come from places such as Whitehall, Kensington Palace and Hampton Court, courtesy of Charles, the Sixth Earl of Dorset. He was able to restock Knole, after parliamentary sacking, with priceless furniture and other valuable objects from the Royal Palaces when he became Lord Chamberlain to William III.

15. THE CARTOON GALLERY. KNOLE.

Copyright – Geo. P. King Ltd. Sevenoaks.

Knole House from N. Sevenoaks.

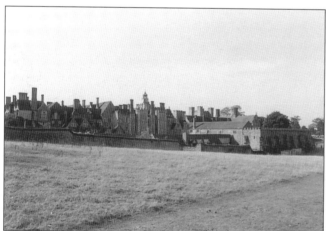

Chancellor and Archbishop of Canterbury, Cardinal Thomas Bourchier, from William, Baron of Say and Sele for £266 13s 4d. Building of the Knole House we know today was begun in 1456 on the site of the previous house, and it lasted until Bourchier's death in 1486. The house was bequeathed to the See of Canterbury, where it saw four more Archbishops until Archbishop Cranmer gave it to Henry VIII. Although he did invest in the house, he didn't live there. Knole eventually passed to Elizabeth I, who in turn gave it to her cousin Thomas Sackville, the First Earl of Dorset, in 1566. It was Sackville who was responsible for the transformation of the house into the magnificent stately home seen today.

A house has stood at Knole since 1291, though not in the form one can see today. The house is set on a 'knoll' meaning higher ground. It was purchased in 1456 by the Lord

Many alterations and additions were made by Sackville between 1603 and his death in 1608. The interior was transformed, with the addition of panelling and plasterwork in the principal rooms. He also installed the Great Staircase. The builders Lord Burghly and Sir Christopher Hatton said that mansions like Knole were built largely to accommodate the Queen, although in this case it has been for descendants of Sackville, who remain in residence today. Knole has been known as a 'Calendar House', because it has 365 rooms, 7 courtyards and 52 staircases. Whilst under control of the Fourth Earl of Dorset, Knole was sacked by Parliamentarian troops in 1642 and again in 1645, losing many treasures. However, when the Fifth Earl married the heiress Lady Frances Cranfield, many fine items were brought to Knole from the Cranfield family home Copt Hall. Knole was further restocked by the Sixth Earl from royal palaces when he became Lord Chancellor to William III.

KNOLE, SEVENOAKS.

During the eighteenth century, the Third Duke of Dorset, known as a romantic, ensured that Knole did not undergo any remodelling in the classical style, which was a fate to befall many stately homes at the time. The house at this time covered approximately four acres. In 1887, all the modifications by Thomas Sackville, and the good intentions of the Third Duke, could have been in vain when a fire broke out at Knole. Three hundred tons of hay, which had been in the side barn, caught alight, with the very real danger of it spreading to the house. The alarm was raised by the Rector of Seal, who rode to the fire station on seeing the smoke. By the time the firemen reached the house, they discovered that the town's volunteer brigade were already there with their 'Ready' fire engine. Between the two groups, they kept the fire from spreading and eventually brought it under control, narrowly averting a disaster.

Probably the best known resident of Knole was Victoria Mary Sackville-West, otherwise known as Vita Sackville-West, daughter of Lionel, the Third Lord Sackville. She was born and brought up at Knole, though in later years moved to Sissinghurst Castle, creating the world-renowned gardens there. In 1913 she married the diplomat and literary critic Harold Nicolson, moving with him on his overseas duties. She was both a poet and novelist, her best known novels being *The Edwardians* (1930) and *All Passion Spent* (1931). In her poem *The Land* (1926) much is made of her closeness to the countryside, no doubt inspired by the surroundings of Knole. The historical fantasy *Orlando* (1928) by Virginia Woolf, a friend of Vita Sackville-West, was set at Knole and came about from their friendship. The original manuscript of the book is on display at the house.

Knole House, West Front, Sevenoaks.   2906.

Charles, the Fourth Lord Sackville, and uncle to Vita, passed care of Knole House to the National Trust in 1946, along with an endowment. This was greeted with anger by Vita Sackville-West. However, he did retain the right to live in certain sections of the house which would not be open to members of the public. The contents of the house and the park itself remain the property of the Sackville family. The house is still run by the National Trust and is open daily throughout the months April to October. It is the most popular tourist attraction of the town, and also has gardens with limited opening times to the public from May to September.

Knole Park is set in one thousand acres of beautiful countryside. Herds of deer roam free, and ancient chestnuts, beeches and oaks abound. The park has had many uses other than simply for recreation. When the threat of war with France and possible invasion arose in 1860, the formation of a volunteer rifle corps necessitated the need for somewhere to carry out target practice. Knole Park was the solution, and the corps used their Enfield rifles in the deep valley of the park. Ordnance maps referred to this valley as the 'volunteer rifle range' for long after. In 1884 Lord Sackville decided that it was time to review the access rules regarding the passage across the park to nearby Godden Green, and proposed new regulations. This did not go down well with the public, and there was quite a

protest. There was a procession through the town, which culminated in the burning of wood taken from the gateway in front of the house.

The entrance gate into Knole leads into the volunteer rifle range referred to previously. This is the bed of an ancient river which was formed after the Ice Age. This river flowed into the nearby River Darent. Opposite this entrance is Ice House Hill.

Glass was once made in the park, during the sixteenth century when the Lennards resided here. Accounts dated 1585 show that wood from the park was sold to the glass-makers in return for glass to be used in the house. Troops descended upon the park again during World War One, when thousands poured into the town after new armies and reserves were formed. Many large camps were set up at Knole to accommodate them.

The manned entrance gate is the main route into Knole Park by vehicle, and it is a short drive from here up to Knole House.

Of all the places to be affected in the area by the great hurricane on the night of 15/16 October 1987, Knole Park was particularly badly hit. Chestnut Walk, which adjoins the Broad Walk seen here, was devastated. Trees were literally torn from their roots and tossed about. Broad Walk was also affected, and in all, about twenty thousand tonnes of trees were uprooted. An appeal was soon up and running in an attempt to replenish the loss. A 'Trees for the Future' appeal in December 1987 replanted seventy local sites, including Knole. The damage of the hurricane can still be seen today, though much has been done to remove the fallen trees and continue the programme of replanting.

The King Beech was situated two hundred and fifty yards from the bottom of the Duchess' Walk in Knole Park, close to where the footpath led to Sevenoaks. It was the largest beech in England, and was thought to date from the sixteenth century.

Its circumference was nearly twenty nine foot, and it was so large the head of the tree was said to be about four times the size of a normal beech. The size of the tree caused problems when high winds blew, which was often the case in Knole Park. When the Countess De La Wall lived at Knole, the boughs were tied to each other by iron rods to give some protection from the wind. King Beech was in the near vicinity of Old Oak another historic tree of the park. Both trees feature on an Ordnance Survey map of 1937, but the beech was felled by April 1946, and the Old Oak

KING BEECH

destroyed by vandals in 1954. The contemporary photograph shows the general area where King Beech once stood.

Knole Park was much smaller than the one seen today when Cardinal Bourchier enclosed it in 1456. Henry VIII and subsequent owners of Knole added small pockets of land piecemeal style until it reached approximately one thousand acres. Herds of Japanese Sika and fallow deer graze throughout the ancient woodlands and valleys of the park, and are always a popular sight amongst visitors. The deer have the added benefit of keeping down the enormous area of grass.

Parts of the park were at one time arable. Under the ownership of the Fifth Earl of Dorset, four farmers were allowed to plough anywhere in the park, except directly in front of the house.

Chapter 2
CHURCHES

During recent archaeological excavations, early foundations were discovered of a church on this site dating from Saxon times. The earliest records of the parish church of St Nicholas date back to 1122 when the church paid its dues to Rochester Cathedral, and burials have been found dating from the twelfth century. The church dates mainly from the thirteenth century, although most of it was rebuilt in the fifteenth century. To the south-east of the church, the building of the chantry chapel came about from an endowment in 1257 by the rector, Henry de Gandavo. Otherwise known as Henry of Ghent, he was the church's third rector, although he was absent from the area for much of the time, appointing a vicar to carry out normal parish duties.

PARISH CHURCH, SEVENOAKS

St. Nicholas Parish Church, Sevenoaks.

A tower was added at the church's north-west corner later in the thirteenth century, as was a south aisle. In the fourteenth century the north aisle was enlarged. However, the church soon fell into disrepair, and by the early part of the fifteenth century the rector was ordered to make important repairs to the chancel. From 1616 until his death in 1631, the poet John Donne, also Dean of St Paul's Cathedral, was rector here. Like Henry of Ghent, however, he too appointed a vicar to carry out normal parish duties and rarely visited the church. He was however, a frequent visitor to Knole.

The church again fell into a state of disrepair by the early nineteenth century. The passing of an Act of Parliament in 1811 allowed for fundraising to repair the damage. The following year, repairs and modifications were made by S.P. Cockerell. This included the addition of clerestory windows, crenellated battlements and a rebuilding of the top stage of the tower. The cost of this restoration was £10,000. As the church was out of action during this time, the nearby Oddfellows Hall was used for services as it had the largest available room in the town. Weddings were held at other nearby churches. Further extensive restorations took place in 1878, which resulted in many changes to the interior. In 1947, the church was

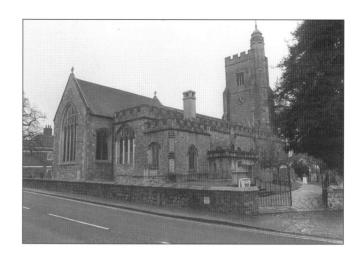

badly damaged when the nave caught alight. However, the damage was soon repaired. In 1966, the eight church bells were re-tuned, costing £4,450.

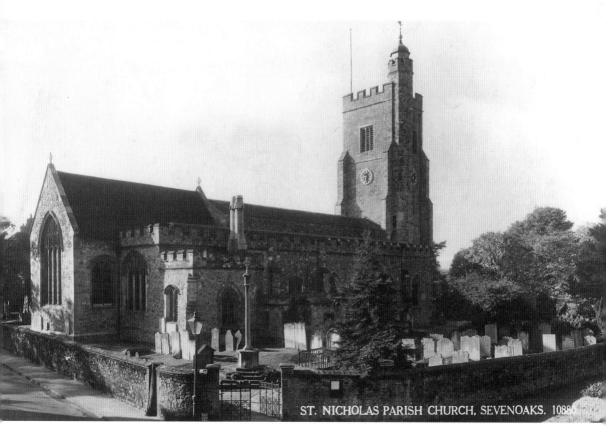

ST. NICHOLAS PARISH CHURCH, SEVENOAKS. 10880

At the turn of the twentieth century, the northern end of the High Street was undergoing rapid development as the town continued to grow. The opening of The Drive was a significant part of this development, with many new houses being built, increasing the size of the community substantially. The Methodists had been using the tiny chapel in Bank Street which they had long outgrown. To ease the burden, a local benefactor, Henry Swaffield, contributed £5,030 to the total cost of £7,640 9s 9d of a new Methodist church. Swaffield wanted the church's design to be similar to that of the Wesleyan church at St Leonard's. In March 1903 work began, and two months later memorial stones were laid. The church was built using local ragstone with Bath stone dressings, and was opened on 9 March 1904. Mrs Swaffield was due to perform the opening ceremony, but this was carried out by Mr Swaffield himself on his wife's behalf. The service was conducted by the Revd Marshall Hartley, President of the Methodist Conference.

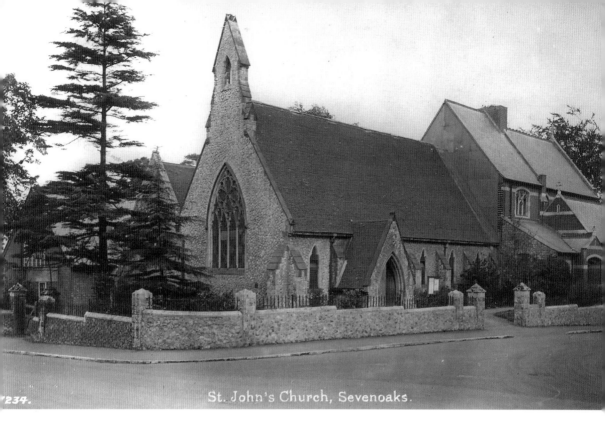

St. John's Church, Sevenoaks.

234.

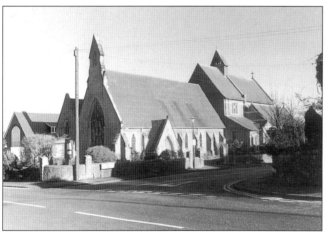

As the development of the town increased in the mid-nineteenth century, developments crept further and further away from the High Street. At the same time, developments were creeping up from Bradbourne Vale Road at the other end of the town. One such area of development was on St John's Hill, linking Bradbourne Vale Road with the High Street. A church was needed in this area, and so one was built on St John's Hill, taking the name of the ancient hospital of St John the Baptist. St John's was opened as a chapel to St Nicholas' church in 1858. It was built by Morpew and Green, and a north aisle was added in 1878. An attempt was made to rebuild the church on a much larger scale in 1901, with the addition of a chancel and vestries. The modifications can be seen in these photographs.

This view from Dartford Road to the western side of St John's church shows several modifications since 1910. Firstly, the bell has been removed from the top of the church. The gateway has also been blocked off and a wall now takes its place. Access is now from the south side along Quakers Hall Lane. The trees have also been removed. As can be seen from the old photograph, these were starting to seriously encroach on the church, restricting the light to the stained glass windows.

The church now has a cleaner, uncluttered look and serves the congregation well.

St. John's Church, Sevenoaks.

ST. MARY'S CHURCH. KIPPINGTON. SEVENOAKS. 4811.

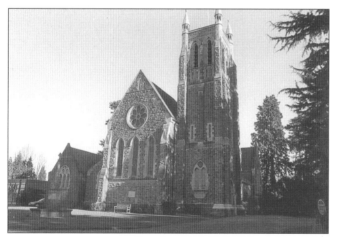

St. Mary's church, on the exclusive Kippington Road, was built on land purchased by the tea merchant Mr William James Thompson. Thompson was also the founder of the Sevenoaks Water Co. and a governor of Sevenoaks School. Thompson bought Kippington House and the adjoining land of some 268 acres from the Austen family in 1854 for £55,000. An active churchwarden at St Nicholas' church, Thompson fell out with the rector, the Revd Thomas Samuel Curteis, over radical changes the new rector had made to the church. The new church was deemed necessary on account of the growing population of the town. New parish boundaries were drawn up for Kippington, based on the old limits of the Kippington estate. The church was built soon after and finally consecrated on 14 June 1880.

The picturesque church of St Bartholomew dates from around 1060, superseding an earlier timber building. The squat, western tower was added around 1180-90. The oldest parts of the church are the north and west walls of the nave, but many alterations have been made to the original building. In the early fourteenth century, the former chancel was replaced by the present one. A south aisle, with the Lady Chapel, and clergy vestry were built in 1520-1530. A fire badly damaged the church in 1630 but major reconstruction work was carried out. Three years later, using the design of the architect G.E. Street, the arcade and chancel–arch were also added.

Church and Pond Otford Kent

FORD FROM THE CHURCH TOWER. 27

The timber broach spire dates from the
seventeenth century. The tower used to
house two bells, which were originally
placed in 1622 and 1674. They were
recast in 1887 and 1975 respectively.
However, since November 2000, the
church now boasts six bells; four of
which were cast at Whitechapel. The
extra weight necessitated the building of
a new frame construction to house all six
bells. They are dedicated to the memory
of a local resident, Joan Dickinson.
Otford pond, seen here, is a focal point
of the village and was provided by the
local benefactor Lord Amherst. Its
general upkeep over the years has mainly
been thanks to the work of the Otford
Preservation Society.

This view is from the tower of St
Bartholomew church. The tower is
accessed through a twelfth century arch,
and the walls at the tower's base are
upwards of four and a half feet thick.

St John's Evangelical church was situated on London Road in Dunton Green. It was built in 1889-90, by M. Potter of Sevenoaks, at a cost of £1,900. The church was built of red brick for the nave and lower chancel, and also bath stone, with a slate roof. Inside the church was carefully textured brickwork. It served the local community well but in the 1970s the congregation started to dwindle. By the early 1980s, the regular congregation was as low as ten, and at this time talks began as to what other uses the church could be put to. The church soon closed its doors and today it is the premises of an antiques restoration business, called Timothy Long Restoration

St. John's Church, Dunton Green, Dunton.

Penshurst Church, Kent.

The parish church of St John the Baptist stands just beyond the area known as Leicester Square. A church may have originally stood on this site as early as AD 860, but was definitely in place by the twelfth century. It is made of sandstone and has an unusual tower, which has stood in this form since the seventeenth century. The tower has eight bells, two of which were originally cast in 1470. Many modifications were made to the church as well as the tower during the seventeenth century. In 1630 a walled aisle was rebuilt along with a north aisle. Later that century the church was systematically looted by Parliamentarians, but much of the property was replaced in 1660 on restoration of the Monarchy. The famous Sidney Chapel dates from 1820, and in 1854 further modifications were made to the interior. The main change to the exterior has been the re-positioning of the clock further up the tower, presumably to make it more visible.

This class of pupils were from one of the infants' schools in the town when they posed for the photographer around 1900. At the start of the nineteenth century, Sevenoaks had two charitable schools, Sevenoaks School and Lady Boswell's School. (Sevenoaks School is discussed in the next few pages.) Lady Boswell's School was founded by Margaret Bosville, who left an endowment for a school upon her death in 1682. The endowment was to teach fifteen of the town's poorest children and also to provide two scholarships of twelve pounds a year to

Chapter 3
EDUCATION

Jesus College, Cambridge. In the 1830s, public elementary schools were provided to cater for the needs of poorer children. Some schools were also provided by wealthy families in the area.

Sevenoaks School, a mainstay of the town for many years, was first established by William Sevenoke. The establishment of the school was in two stages. In 1418 he established a free school within his own house, and in 1432 he endowed it and a hospital for the poor. The story of Sevenoke is that he was found as an abandoned child in the town, and later became a wealthy merchant in London. Later still he became Mayor of London, preceding his friend Richard Whyttington (Dick Whittington). However, this story has been much embellished. The school building as seen here was built to replace other buildings between 1724-1734, and was designed by Lord Burlington, a leading architect. The building was extended by the addition of a new storey on the southern side around 1875, and further extension of the existing storey to the north. The purpose of this was to attract more pupils to the school. The statue in the centre of the building in the new photograph is of William Sevenoke.

This view of the old school house is taken from the back of the building, in the school grounds. The school house is now known as Old School, and no longer serves as a boarding house. New accommodation for boarders who used to use the school house has now been secured in nearby Oak Lane. Old School is now used by the Mathematics Centre. One Old Boy of the school was John Frith. Born in nearby Westerham, he went on to Eton and Cambridge. He was famous for helping to translate the New Testament into English. However, other workings of his were denounced as heresy and he went to the stake at the age of thirty-one.

For centuries the school remained

small and had a solely local focus. This was to change, however, in the twentieth century as the school sought to attract pupils from further afield.

evenoaks School. School House (the Headmaster's Boarding House).

Then two photographs show the dramatic changes which have been made to the school over the last century. The old photograph shows the school house on the right, the assembly hall and gymnasium in the centre, and the laboratory and workshops on the left, which were added in 1900. On the far right of the new photograph is the Johnson Hall built around 1935, and now used as the school library, which houses over twenty-seven thousand books. The foreground is dominated by the Marley Sports Centre, built in 1977. The Marley Centre is used for such sports as football, cricket and basketball. It also contains a gym and at certain times of the year the hall is used for public exams. The new building behind the Marley Centre was built in 2000 on the site of the old dining block to provide additional facilities for the school. It houses the departments of Art and Modern Languages while also providing dining facilities.

School pupils have changed completely since the school was established, and even more so over the last century. The school pupils shown here were known as 'toppers and Eton collars' at the time of the photograph, around 1880. The new photograph shows pupils from a typical fifth form class. The school now has many international students, mainly because it is one of the few British schools to teach exclusively for the International Baccalaureate diploma in the Sixth Form. Today, there are approximately nine hundred and sixty pupils in the school. A third of the pupils are boarders, and there are almost as many girls now as boys.

Walthamstow Hall, Sevenoaks.

Walthamstow Hall was built in 1882, and at this time it was both the largest and the most expensive building in the town. It was built at a cost of £22,000 and is one of the oldest girls' schools in the country, founded in 1838. It was originally the 'School for Missionaries' Daughters', for daughters of missionaries serving abroad. The school had relocated from Walthamstow after a local resident, the founder's daughter, had recommended the clean air and countryside. When the school opened in the town, the school began accepting day pupils. Today it is an independent school with approximately four hundred and fifty pupils between the ages of three and eighteen years. The school's emblem is a ship, which is to signify the importance of ships in allowing the parents of the early pupils to carry out their missionary duties overseas.

There are many sporting clubs and teams in the Sevenoaks District. Football, cricket and bowling in particular are popular. There are many leisure facilities in the area, including tennis courts, swimming pools, athletic tracks, squash courts and of course outdoor pitches for rugby, football and cricket. This photograph shows Seal Football Club around 1900 or possibly even earlier. Presumably the team members standing actually wore long shorts as was usual for the time. The long-sleeved button-up football shirts are distinctive with their matching collars and breast pockets.

Chapter 4
AT WORK AND PLAY

Sevenoaks Town Band was formed in 1890 after a public meeting was held that year at the Lime Tree Hotel. At the inaugural meeting, twenty-two men enrolled as paying members; each paid the sum of 15s to the band's treasury. Soon after the band's formation, Henry Swaffield - who helped to build the New Methodist church – took an interest and provided the band with a building to serve as their own practice and meeting place. He also provided them with a bandstand. Both of these were built on the Vine Cricket Ground and still exist today. Over the years, the band has played at many town functions, including Christmas Concerts, the Town Fayre, at the Stag Theatre, Knole, and the Cricket Club. They have visited Pontoise, twin town of Sevenoaks, and also played at the appeal concert after the hurricane of 1987. Today the band do not wear the formal dress as seen in the old photograph taken on the Vine in 1925, preferring white shirt and blue tie.

The Smithy at Penshurst used to be home to the local blacksmith. The old photograph shows the smith, John Ephraim Skinner, with the iron fire-screen which he made and which was subsequently presented to Sevenoaks Museum by Mr Hills of Penshurst. John Skinner was a skilled blacksmith and farrier, and on 31 December 1900 he received his Certificate of Registration into the Worshipful Company of Farriers. The smithy, built in 1891, is a famous local landmark, and it appears on many postcards. This is mainly because it is one of the few remaining horseshoe smithy's in existence. Today it has many uses, that of petrol station and workshop, post

office and convenience store. The new photograph shows Ian Streeter dispensing petrol to a customer.

The old photograph shows the Sevenoaks Cycling Club posing outside the Lime Tree Temperance Hotel in 1886. By 1907, the hotel had become a thriving centre for many cycling clubs in the area, and home to the Sevenoaks Cycling Club. Around this time the area was swamped each weekend with gentlemen and their new toys, 'Penny Farthings', tricycles and the new 'safety' pedal bikes. At the entrance to Lime Tree Walk, on which the hotel stood, was a local bike builder, Timberlake. The hotel was damaged by a bomb in 1940. Cycling is still popular in the town, and each Saturday, members of the West Kent Association of the Cyclists' Touring Club meet at the railway station for their weekly ride.

The photograph below, from the beginning of the twentieth century, shows workmen with their steam roller dressed in waistcoat, flat cap, and work trousers. As was common for the time, there was no regard for personal safety. Compare that with the typical workman of today. Firstly, their vehicle has flashing lights to warn others. Cones are liberally used to mark off dangerous or working areas. The workmen now wear luminous vests so as to be clearly seen, hard hats for head protection, and safety boots for protection from the heavy equipment they use. They also have use of 'walkie-talkies' for instant and easy communication. In this case,

ear defenders are also used due to the noise level of the equipment in treating the tarmac.

Several Bowling Clubs have been in existence in this area for around a hundred years. It was a popular pastime amongst the more well-heeled generation. The old photograph shows members of Brasted Bowling Club around 1900. The club is still going today, though has merged with another local club and is now called the Sundridge and Brasted Bowling Club and has approximately fifty. The new photograph shows members of the Sevenoaks Bowling Club, which celebrates its ninetieth year in 2001, having been formed in 1911. An affiliate of the English Bowling Association, and Kent County Bowling Association, the club still uses its original clubhouse. It has two greens, which are rented from Sevenoaks District Council. Current membership stands at approximately eighty-five men, forty ladies, and forty social members. Formal dress is still worn, with whites and blazers on match day. The main difference from 1900 is the inclusion of ladies to bowling clubs.

The First Sevenoaks (Hicks Own) Scout Group was established in 1909, just one year after Baden-Powell formed the scout movement. It was established by Bill Hicks in April of that year, and his first scouts were pupils of Lady Boswell's School, where he was a teacher. The first meeting place of the scouts was the Parish Room of St Nicholas, but this later moved to the Manor House, part of Sevenoaks School. The old photograph dates from 1920 and shows the group during its presentation of colours at camp. The group has had a chequered history, barely surviving World War One, not helped by the death of Hicks in France on 3 July 1917. The club managed better through World War Two, and by the 1950s there was a waiting list

for the cub side. By the 1970s the club was thriving, with the Headquarters being used by Cubs, Scouts, Venture Scouts, Brownies and Guides. The new photograph shows cubs at a recent camp held in Guernsey.

Sevenoaks Town Football Club has a distinguished history in the town, having been established in 1894. As can be seen from the old photograph, success came early with the winning of a trophy six years later, during the 1900-01 season. The football club is still going strong. They currently play home games at Greatness Park, off Seal Road. They are well supported by fans and the ubiquitous sponsor. They play in the British Energy Premiership Divison and in 2000 they won the Sevenoaks Charity Cup in the Senior Section. The reserves also won the Junior Section of the same cup.

Ide Hill Cricket Club has also been in existence since 1894. The old dress of shirt tie and waistcoat has given way to the usual whites of today. The club does not participate in a league, but rather plays friendly games with other local clubs, such as those at Chiddingstone, Buckhurst and Toys Hill. There is a local competition which the clubs participate in for the Local Clerk Trophy. Their home ground is at the National Trust owned Emmett's Park. The cricket pitch was left to the club by a previous owner of Emmett's, a Mr Boyce. The club currently has approximately thirty

members, and fields one team from this squad twice a week during the cricket season.

47

engine was bought for the brigade through public subscription. When the fire engine was delivered, the town held a celebration. The Tonbridge Town Band escorted the new fire engine up Tubs Hill, drawn by four horses and holding the men of the brigade. At the fountain at the top of the High Street, the engine was christened 'Ready' by the daughter of the captain, Mr W.H. Stepney. In 1887 the Brigade put out a fire at Knole using this engine. It was also used to quell the fire at Mr Essenhigh-Corke's photographic studio. The volunteer brigade was disbanded in 1894. In 1972 the fire brigade moved to a new complex at Morewoods on London Road, where they are today. The new photograph shows the current brigade alongside their newest fire tender.

Sevenoaks had a volunteer brigade to be proud of. It was established in 1820 by the Board of Guardians, and it used the same fire engine until 3 January 1883. At this time, a new 'Ready' fire

Chapter 5
PUBS AND HOTELS

During the sixteenth century, the increase in population of the town meant new settlements sprang up on the outskirts, normally at existing road junctions or farmhouses. One such settlement was that of Godden Green, just north of Knole Park. It has a relaxed atmosphere, with the expanse of common to the right and the popular Buck's Head pub on the left. Adding to the tranquil scene is the fenced off pond in front of the pub. In the summer, the area heaves with people, and hikers find the pub a good location for a snack and a drink. The area has barely changed over the last one hundred years, except for the cars parked down one side of the road today.

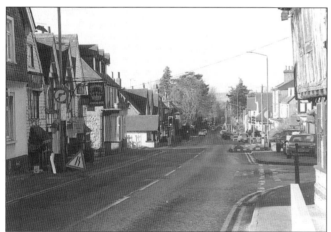

Two pubs fight for business in Seal, The Crown Inn and the Kentish Yeoman. The Kentish Yeoman is behind The Crown Inn several doors further down the road. The old photograph was probably taken in the first decade of the twentieth century, and both pubs are still going strong today. On the right, where the tree stands in the old photograph, was the village forge. Today a car salesroom occupies the site. This road was not tar surfaced until 1909, and was made up of hard packed dirt and stone until this time. Once it had been tar surfaced, there were calls for a speed limit of ten miles per hour to be introduced. Today, it is a busy road, especially during week days. It forms part of the A25, carrying traffic to and from Maidstone

The Leicester Arms is the only pub actually in the small and peaceful village of Penshurst, but there are others on its outskirts. The pub was once called The Porcupine, which was the creature used on the Sidney Family crest. The sign hanging outside the pub holds the motto of the Order of the Garter, surrounding the pheon (head of a dart or arrow) of the Sidney emblem. It says 'Honi Soit Qui Mal Y Pense', meaning 'Shame to him who thinks evil (of it)'. The name was changed to the Leicester Arms but this still has links with the Sidney family, who were Earls of Leicester. The first Earl of Leicester was Sir Robert Sidney in 1616. The pub is a prime example

of solid Elizabethan workmanship, with exposed oak beams and an old fireplace.

The White Hart Hotel is the first public house encountered on the entry to Sevenoaks from the south. The hotel started off as a pub and farmhouse, servicing travellers who ran stage coaches between London and the south coast. This journey used to take two days and so a break at this peaceful location overlooking Knole Park was well deserved. The weary travellers could stop off, stock up on food and drink, and change their horses. The White Hart also has a secluded and manicured garden, which is best appreciated in the summer. The stable area to the left of the hotel has for many years been the White Hart Garage, selling Citroën cars. The seven oaks are still located here, just to the left of the garage out of sight. The oaks standing there today were planted in 1955 to replace the old ones which were felled in 1954.

The Royal Oak Hotel, opposite Sevenoaks School, was originally called the Black Bull. This view is from the garden to the rear. The façade was re-fronted in ragstone around 1820. Many other changes have occurred to this building over the last century. The most noticeable of which is that part of the building to the right has been demolished. In its place, is the Royal Oak Tap public house. Between the two buildings is now a driveway giving access to the rear where a car park has replaced the neatly manicured lawns. The hotel has also been extended to the rear, and extra accommodation units have been built to the rear of the car park. The hotel now boasts thirty seven

individually designed bedrooms, conference facilities, restaurant, bistro and conservatory.

THE ROYAL OAK, SEVENOAKS.

53

Royal Crown Hotel, Sevenoaks.

The Royal Crown was a mainstay of the town for over 150 years, situated on the corner of South Park with London Road. It was a popular resting place in the nineteenth century for travellers between London and the south coast. It had an enormous ballroom which played host to many town functions and also the annual Grand Ball for the hotel's staff and servants. The hotel also had extensive gardens, which included a vegetable garden, miniature farm breeding pigs and chickens, and an aviary; all provided for the guests. At the South Park end of the hotel stood the Royal Crown Tap. In the early part of the twentieth century, the hotel was closed down and sold. It stood in an almost derelict state for some years before it was finally demolished in 1932 to make way for another cinema, the fourth in the town. The Stag theatre and cinema now stands on the London Road side, and on the South Park side stands the post office, built in 1975.

Sevenoaks was almost as famous for its pubs as it was for its seven oak trees. The High Street was packed with pubs, the majority of which have now been taken over as other commercial interests. One such pub was the Oddfellows and Foresters' Arms, seen in the old photograph around 1890. This small pub was in existence in 1880 and proved to be a popular watering hole, especially in the early part of the twentieth century. However, it shut its doors for the last time in the late 1960s, and in 1969 was an off licence called Victoria Wine. As a sign of the times, it is now a mobile phone retail outlet called the Mobile Phone Centre.

wall of the brewery still in existence. Blighs was originally a farmhouse dating from the sixteenth century, and belonging to the Archbishop of Canterbury. In the eighteenth century the building was rented by the Bethlehem Hospital for the Insane. At this time it was known as Bethlehem or Bedlam Farm. The name Blighs was adopted when John Bligh bought the property in 1882. He ran it as a house and a hotel; the house stood on the left and the hotel to the right. Bligh was a successful local businessman, owning several public houses in addition to his main occupation as a brewer. His brewery was known as the Holmesdale Brewery. Blighs is still a popular public house but is no longer run as an hotel.

Another High Street public house is Blighs Hotel, at the northern end of the High Street. The original photograph was taken in 1903, with the

This area of the town, at the bottom of Tubs Hill, is where the main Sevenoaks Railway Station is situated. The public house on the left is the Railway and Bicycle, and the railway station lies just beyond it. The public house on the right was known as The Sennocke Arms or Sennocke Hotel for many years, until it changed its name to the more modern The Farmers. Known as Station Parade, there are a row of shops on the right before The Farmers, but the garage and taxi rank in the old photograph have long gone. There is now a fish and chip shop, newsagents, estate agents and the like in their place. Taxis still ply their trade but they now have reserved spaces in the small car park outside the railway station.

2595. STATION PARADE, SEVENOAKS.

Looking down London Road, with the fountain behind, many changes have occurred in this scene over the last one hundred years. The most noticeable is that the Royal Crown Hotel on the corner of South Park is no longer there, having been demolished in 1932. It has since been replaced by the Stag theatre and post office. On the right, and undergoing final stages of renovation in the new photograph, is the Chequers Inn. A listed building, this was built in the sixteenth century on the site of an earlier inn. It was originally a coaching inn where three coaches used to stop each week on the journey to Maidstone and London. On the extreme right is the building of the HSBC Bank.

Chapter 6

HIGH STREET

According to the note on the postcard, this view of 1906 looks out over the town from the High Street, although from exactly where is not certain. The scene is dominated by vegetation, with a couple of buildings poking out from the undergrowth. Sevenoaks still has woodland left, although intense development from the eighteenth and nineteenth centuries, to cater for the ever increasing population, has meant that much woodland has been cleared. The centre of the town is now packed with residential and commercial premises, but there are still wooded areas such as Wildernesse, Knole, Sevenoaks Common and Great Britain's Wood.

This area of the Upper High Street is the first commercial area encountered when arriving at Sevenoaks from the south, along the Tonbridge Road. The road bends sharply to the left where it goes out of sight, and just around this corner is an entrance to Sevenoaks School and beyond that is Knole Park. The building in the middle of the photograph is the Royal Oak Hotel and to the left of it is the Royal Oak Tap. The town's old post office can be seen on the extreme right. Between the old post office and the Royal Oak are old residential cottages and Oak Lane. To the left are the almshouses of Sevenoaks School. The school itself is just out of the picture. This area of the town has hardly changed over the last century, with the exception that it can become a bottleneck when rush hour traffic arrives during the week.

The old post office was built in the fifteenth century, and was once part of a larger hall house, or possibly a town house of one of the outlying manors. At some time it was split into three separate buildings. Over the years it has been a house, an inn and a shop, for which it is most well known. The building has some eighteenth and nineteenth century sliding windows, which were a cheaper alternative to sash or casement windows. It also has two types of decorative tile-hanging which were added later to hide the timber frame. It is now a newsagents, popular amongst residents at this end of the town, and ever popular with pupils of Sevenoaks School just over the road.

The aptly named White House was for many years an antique dealers. It may have been Tudor in origin, although it was almost completely rebuilt in 1840. The new façade never really blended into its surroundings. It is said that the building had secret tunnels running from here along to St Nicholas' church. The antique dealers Martin & Dolton had moved into the White House from the current Woolworths site in the 1920s, and soon before he died, Mr Dolton sold the house to another antiques dealer, Rupert Samuelson. Samuelson, wanted to demolish the grade II listed building, and in 1963 appealed against the preservation order. At the appeal, the Government Inspector was advised by experts that there was nothing wrong with the structure, and that the order should be maintained. However, the inspector found otherwise, stating that dry rot and death-watch beetle infestation had taken hold. The building was finally demolished in the early 1970s. On the site now stands an opticians and a bicycle shop.

Occupying Nos 63 to 65 in the High Street, at the junction with London Road, is Outrams. The shop is named after James Outram, who opened up his leather goods business in the town during the latter part of the nineteenth century in opposition to Ellimanns further down the High Street. Although hung with nineteenth century fish-scale tiles, the premises were built in the fifteenth century and served as the principal residence for the Reeve or Agent of the Archbishop of Canterbury. There is still a Tudor fireplace which has the coat of arms of both Archbishop Chichele and Archbishop Warham carved into it. The founder died in 1927, but the shop remained a feature of the town until 2001. The owner decided to retire and subsequently he sold the business. At the time of writing, Outrams was holding a closing down sale. It is due to be replaced by a fish restaurant.

This corner of Bank Street and No. 101 High Street, has undergone many changes over the years. The Sevenoaks Clothing Company was a popular business and was operating here in the late nineteenth century. The reason for its popularity was no doubt because it provided Sevenoaks with its first discount clothing store, selling a wide variety of items. The premises were later owned by the company Gower and White, and later still became a butchers shop. The last butcher to operate here was a Mr Malpas. The present occupiers are the estate agents and chartered surveyors, Millest and Partners. On the extreme right can be seen part of the Market House, dating from 1843 but replacing an earlier building of Tudor times. This building has undergone many changes of use, including market place, corn exchange, court house and technical institute. It is now home to a hairdressing salon.

The old photograph on the High Street, taken around 1875, shows two of the most well known shops at the time. These were Elliman's Royal Embrocation, owned by Mr Gandy, and the basket makers, owned by Mr Amos Pett. Elliman's sold brushes, sponges, saddles, tack and other leather goods. He was firmly established in the High Street by the time James Outram opened up his leather goods shop in opposition. Mr Pett was a quality basket maker who took an active involvement in the local institutions. These shops are opposite what is Woolworths. Mr Pett's later became a branch of the Freeman Hardy

Willis shoe retail chain. Today the shops are run by a health business and a charity.

Opposite the shops of Elliman's and Pett's, stood Dunn the butchers, and Parris', the patisserie and confectioner. Parris' moved further along the High Street in the 1930s to open a new, larger shop, comprising of restaurant serving teas, dinners and luncheons. It continued to serve as a patisserie and confectioner, and was quite plush for its time. The delivery horses and carriages for both shops are awaiting their orders in the old photograph, taken around the turn of the twentieth century. Woolworths has occupied this site for a number of years now, and the original weather board buildings along this part of the High Street have been replaced by more functional twentieth century designs.

H.E Warren's was a popular jewellers in the High Street for many years. The old photograph here shows the shop dwarfed by the scaffolding work going on next door. Due to this rebuilding work Warren's had moved next door temporarily, as can be seen by the sign 'temporary premises'. This rebuilding took place in at the beginning of the nineteenth century. The timber-framed temporary premises have long been replaced by a grander structure. This is now occupied by Leslie Warren, Opticians, a company formed by the son of H.E Warren. The clock was added to the building several years later, and restored in the 1980s.

Although many buildings still remain in this scene, the modifications and rebuilding are quite apparent when looking at the skyline. Most noticeable is the modern frontage of what is now the Iceland frozen food store, to the left of centre. This used to be the Rose and Crown Hotel, which was a respectable and prominent business in the early part of the twentieth century. It was quite common for families to take tea in the pleasant surroundings. It finally closed in 1936. The weather boarding has disappeared today and awnings are no longer in operation. The other noticeable difference is the tarred road and the proliferation of cars.

ooking north along the busy Dartford Road, the United Reformed church can just be seen straight ahead. Now forming part of the A225, further north the road drops downhill and becomes St John's Hill, before meeting up with the junction of Bradbourne Vale Road and Seal Road. Dartford Road played an important part in the development of the town, because it linked the developed area to the north around Bradbourne Vale Road, with the High Street to the south. It wasn't until homes were built in this area in the nineteenth century that the town lost its hourglass shape of developments at either end of the road. It is unusual to see Dartford Road quite so deserted as it is in this photograph.

Chapter 7
THOROUGHFARES

DARTFORD Rᴰ LOOKING NORTH, SEVENOAKS.

This scene is looking south towards Raley's Corner, from just in front of the fountain where London Road meets the High Street. It was named Raley's Corner after the baker and pastry chef. The shop which is now on the corner of Six Bells Lane, in the middle of the photograph, used to be a public house called the Six Bells Alehouse. This was named after the peal of six bells from nearby St Nicholas' church. Little has changed in this scene except the replacement of the listed building on the right, The White House, with what is now an opticians and bicycle shop. The other major change is the road junction which can be seen in the foreground. The turning at the stop line takes the driver onto the High Street, and this junction has seen many accidents and near misses since its introduction.

One of the most popular scenes of Sevenoaks is the fountain at the junction of London Road with the High Street. The old photograph is from the late nineteenth century, probably in the 1870s, when the highway was still a dirt road. The building on the foreground bears the name Corke, which was Charles Essinghigh-Corke's photographic studios. Corke was one of the foremost photographers and artists in the area. The fountain was donated in 1882 by an anonymous benefactor. The area behind the fountain stretching down the High Street used to hold a stock market every third Wednesday. The origins of the market go back to the fifteenth century, and today a market is still held in the same place. Corke's studios were taken over in 1900 by the

Sevenoaks Coffee Tavern, which in turn was replaced by the West End Dairy by 1920. Midland Bank took over the premises in 1924, and they still occupy the building today, although it is now the HSBC bank.

The building on the left, in the old market place, is a Lloyds TSB Bank. It used to be residential premises, belonging to the Salmon family of printers and stationers. It opened as Lloyds Bank in 1899, and the old photograph here is from around 1912. The bank was soon doing well and in 1929 decided to take over the adjoining stationers' premises of Salmon's at No. 85 High Street. The bank was subsequently enlarged. One of the town's old pubs, the Rose and Crown, used to occupy the premises now taken over by Iceland, the frozen food chain. The building is on the right hand side and in the old photograph the pub's sign can be seen stretching out into the High Street, behind the horse wagon. The Rose and Crown was a popular pub for many years, taking the overflow of stage coaches from the Royal Crown in London Road. It closed its doors for the last time in 1936.

The Constitutional Club, on the junction of Seal Hollow Road with Dartford Road at the northern end of the High Street, was established with the assistance of Sir Charles Mills. Later to become Lord Hillingdon, he was a banker who bought Wildernesse House in 1886. The club was built in 1889, and soon became a favourite haunt of well-heeled members of the town, who enjoyed the fine facilities the club had to offer, including an excellent quality snooker table. There used to be a hall attached to the club, which at one time was the largest venue available in the town, holding five hundred people. However, in 1940 it was hit by a bomb and destroyed. The Sevenoaks Conservative Club took over the

running for many years, until January 1957 when the club closed. Today it is used as commercial premises called TAG Business Systems.

Sevenoaks, Seal Hollow

Seal Hollow Road has changed little in the last one hundred years. Previously called Locks Bottom Road, it is a long, narrow and winding road which joins the High Street with Seal Road. It lays in a natural river valley, formed after the Ice Age. It is approximately at the northern edge of what was the ancient Forest of Andred, which was a dark and foreboding place until Saxon settlers began clearing it. The narrowness of the road can be slightly disconcerting for drivers, and this is highlighted by the wall which bricks off Knole Park. This wall was built in the early nineteenth century by Welsh stonemasons. Beyond the trees and to the right of this scene is the Vine Cricket Ground.

Looking eastwards towards Maidstone on the A25, it would be suicidal today for any children to be playing in the middle of the road. Ever since the road was tarred in 1909, residents have been calling for speed restrictions. In this respect, little has changed over the last century as this has always been a busy road. On the left, the building in the old photograph was likely to be some type of commercial enterprise. Today it is an Italian restaurant called Grumbles, although it was closed for building work at the time of writing. Further up the hill on the left are a number of commercial premises.

The picturesque Wildernesse Avenue, further north along Seal Hollow Road, was planted in 1815, to commemorate the Battle of Waterloo. It leads to Wildernesse House, which was built by Sir Charles Bickerstaffe in 1669. The house was surrounded by a park of three hundred and sixty four acres. Further modifications were made to the house, especially by Lord Hillingdon in the late nineteenth century. Upon Lady Hillingdon's death in 1921, it became a country club with Wildernesse Golf Club in its grounds.

In 1954 the house was purchased by the Royal London Society for the Blind. It is now known as Dorton House and run as a school and college of further education for the visually impaired.

Looking south along London Road in Riverhead, towards Riverhead church in the background and from the Bull Finch Pub, there used to be an imposing building on the left, known as the Flemish House. The old photograph dates from around 1900, and even at this time it can clearly be seen that the building was not in the best of conditions. The house was linked to the tanyard on the other side of the road, and certainly has the look of an industrial building, with the oversized chimney stack. When the house was finally demolished, a small terrace of residential homes was erected on the site.

This building is thought to have been situated along Vine Court Road, just north of the Vine Cricket Ground off Dartford Road. It is likely that it was demolished at sometime in the mid to late twentieth century to make way for a tranche of new developments which have taken place in that area of the town. This cottage was typical of its time and of the area as a whole. It had the white weather boarding which can still be seen today in the older parts of the town, for instance Six Bells Lane. It also has dormer style windows, another common feature of buildings, especially at the upper end of the High Street near St Nicholas' church.

Chapter 8
AROUND
SEVENOAKS

GODDEN GREEN, SEVENOAKS

The settlement of Godden Green has barely changed since the old photograph was taken in 1906. The tranquil nature of the area is only spoilt by the number of cars which park along the narrow road when visiting the public house called the Bucks Head, on the extreme right. Godden Green is a very small settlement, first established in the sixteenth century as Sevenoaks sought new areas to provide scope for housing in answer to its ever growing population. It is away from the hustle of the town centre, nestled around the far northern end of Knole Park. Knole Park is to the left of picture.

The World War One memorial on Dartford Road came about after a letter to the *Sevenoaks Chronicle* from rector Revd John Rooker in 1919. Revd Rooker suggested 'that a soldier in khaki should be erected on the Vine'. Like most local towns, Sevenoaks was badly affected by the loss of its townsfolk. Two hundred and twenty-five lives were lost in the war. A memorial appeal was quickly launched, and from house to house collections alone, £5,663 was raised. The memorial was unveiled by the owner of Knole House, Lord Sackville, on 29 October 1920. At the unveiling, he said that any surplus funds from the appeal would go the Holmesdale Cottage Hospital. The memorial now also includes an acknowledgement to those lives lost during World War Two.

The Vine Cricket Ground is one of the oldest cricket grounds in England. It was originally used as a vineyard by the Archbishops of Canterbury. The ground eventually came into the hands of the Third Duke of Dorset, owner of Knole. He gave it to the town in 1773. In 1734, the first media reported cricket match took place here. 'The Gentlemen of Kent' beat 'The Gentlemen of Sussex'. The Vine Cricket Club rents the ground from the town council for a peppercorn rent. They, in turn, must pay Lord Sackville one cricket ball on the 21 July each year if requested. The photographs show the western side of the pitch with the band room of the Sevenoaks Town Band. Built in 1890, the band room was partly restored in March 2000 by Sevenoaks Town Council, from whom the band rent the building.

The old photograph shows the Vine Cricket Ground before gardens were added and a bandstand and band room erected for the Sevenoaks Town Band. These were built after the house had been demolished. The Pierce family lived here for many years. It was their privilege on match days to have the best view. The old pitch roller on the right was horse-drawn. In 1918, the ground buzzed with the noise of a World War One bi-plane taking off during the 'help the soldier' appeal. The elms were a feature of the ground until after World War Two. In 1937 the nineteenth century weatherboard cricket pavilion, a listed building, was reconstructed and opened

by Lord Sackville. In 1956 Lord Sackville accepted a cricket ball from the council as nominal rent for the cricket ground.

THE SEVEN OAKS.

The seven oaks, from which the town gets its name, have had a turbulent history. The original oaks were probably near St Nicholas' church. The planting of seven oak trees has only occurred at the vine and near the White Hart Pub over the last two centuries. In 1902, seven oaks were planted on the Vine Cricket Ground, to commemorate the coronation of King Edward VII. On 28 September 1954, the seven oaks which had stood in line on London Road, near the White Hart pub for 127 years, were felled. According to the town council, they were rotten. They may have been wrong; but in March the following year Vita Sackville-West and Miss E. Viner from the council planted seven new saplings from Knole in this location. In October 1987, the great hurricane blew down six of the seven oaks on the Vine Cricket Ground. Overnight Sevenoaks became 'oneoak'. Seven new saplings were planted in their place; but in 1988, almost one year after the hurricane, vandals destroyed the saplings. These were then replaced by more mature trees.

To provide for the increasing population, a fund was set up in 1870 to purchase land and build a hospital. Opened in 1873 the Holmesdale Cottage Hospital had eight beds and one nurse. In its first year, it dealt with thirty-eight patients. It was really no more than a cottage with a few facilities. The hospital was extended in 1904 after a donation for a new ward was made by David Reid. The hospital was well utilised during World War One, but staff shortages did cause problems. After the war, an appeal was made for £28,000 to build a hospital with proper resources. In 1921 all the patients were moved to the Oak Lane Isolation Hospital. During the next year, patients were returned to the rebuilt Holmesdale Hospital, which then had twenty-two

beds. In 1928 a children's ward was added, and in 1933 the name was changed to Sevenoaks and Holmesdale Hospital. Since then, the hospital has been rebuilt and expanded many times. It is now a community hospital.

Six Bells Lane, off the Upper High Street, probably took its name from when St Nicholas' church had a peel of six bells. It now has eight as previously mentioned, but it was not thought necessary to change the name. The row of predominately eighteenth century cottages display typical Kentish weather-boarding, and it is one of the older areas of the town. It appears that the cottages in the centre of the old photograph has been rebuilt or demolished at some time in the twentieth century, probably in the latter half. Apart from this, very little has changed over the last century. The name of the lane had changed to Parsonage Lane, due to the proximity of St Nicholas' church, but this was not a permanent amendment. Six Bells Lane was the site of one of only three water pumps in the town at the end of the nineteenth century.

The Lodge at Hernewood, today known as Hernewood Lodge, lies off Gracious Lane to the west of the town in the Sevenoaks Common area. It was built around 1889 and served as the lodge for the estate of Hernewood, the house of which is further down the drive to the right. Hernewood House has now been modified and today consists of two residential properties. The Lodge has undergone several modifications itself since it was built. The front door has been moved from the left hand side of the building to the right, and it has been extended to the right and to the rear and the chimney was also removed at some point. The ground on which the iron railings and gate were situated now forms part of the adjoining property.

The Lodge, Hernewood, Sevenoaks.

Just off of the High Street is a narrow alley, called Redmans Place. It is one of the older parts of the town, and now leads from the High Street to the bus depot and car park. The old photograph from around 1900 shows the surrounding buildings as all timber framed. The alley runs between Nos 78 and 80, which are now Lorimers and Barclays Bank. In April 1961, the area around Redmans Place was flattened. The alley had an old barn adjoining it, which was used by a market trader to store his fruit boxes. This barn was built on the site of a chapel opened by John Wesley in 1774.

In 1838, Knockholt House was owned by Joseph Skerritt, Lieutenant Colonel of the Thirty-Fifth Regiment, but in 1863 it was bought by James Vavasseur, a wealthy silk merchant and according to local opinion, something of a megalomaniac. He had the house demolished and rebuilt in 1890 and incorporated a revolutionary heating system. A tall tower, which was some thirty-five metres high, was built to support the chimney. Legend has it that Vavasseur kept a boat at the tower in preparation for the next great flood. This photograph was taken in about 1900. After the rebuilding work had been completed. The building looked almost industrial, and had a fully glazed roof which enabled the third floor to be used as a winter garden. The building was finally demolished in 1942 and the remains sold off.

Chapter 9
OUTLYING AREAS

Knockholt House.

The Saxon name of Ightham was *Ehteham* and it is here where a mote stands at the foot of a hill fed by the River Shode. Ightham Mote is a small manor house, parts of which date from 1340. The oldest part is the Great Hall, which was built by Sir William Cawne. It had a crypt which was below the waterline of the mote. It was bought in 1591 by the Selby family, and Sir William Selby was the first to welcome James Stuart to England. The skeleton of Sir William's wife, Dorothy, was said to have been found bricked up in the wall of the Great Hall. The Mote underwent many modifications over the centuries, and it is now a mixture of different styles and materials. Now National Trust property, Ightham Mote has recently undergone an extensive £4,000,000 restoration to highlight its former glories.

Originally built for residential use in 1850, the post office at Penshurst was firmly established by the 1870s. Set in the peaceful south-western corner of historic Leicester Square, the post office remained in the hands of the same family for many years. However, in the early 1980s the post office was moved to another location in the village. The old post office was converted back into residential dwellings.

Except for the change of use of the building, this part of the village has remained largely unchanged over the last century. Penshurst post office is now situated at the petrol station of the old blaksmiths.

The Post Office, Penshurst. No 54.

In 1338 Sir John de Pultney bought Penshurst House and estate. He oversaw the building of the Baron's Hall, built of local sandstone and measuring six hundred feet by thirty-two feet. It is sixty feet high and it took three years to complete. Pultney received a licence to crenellate it in 1341, although this was purely for aesthetic reasons. A further licence was granted in 1393 to fortify the house, and this was carried out after Pultney's death by Sir John Deveraux. Curtain walls and turrets were then added to the house. Since 1552, this stately home has been in the Sidney family. It was at this time that King Edward VI granted it to his tutor, Sir William Sidney. It is still in the Sidney family, as the present owner is Philip Sidney Second Viscount De L'Isle.

Otford, to the north of Sevenoaks, derives its name from *Ottanford*, Anglo-Saxon for Otta's Ford. Although a peaceful and well preserved village, Otford has a bloody history. Two battles have been fought here. The first, around AD 775, occurred when the Anglo-Saxon King Offa of Mercia and his army attacked. They were warded off by the locals, the Kentings. When Offa finally gained control of southern England at the end of the eighth century, he gave lands at Otford to Christ Church, Canterbury. The second battle occurred in 1016 when King Edmund Ironside and his troops saw off King Cnut's (Canute's) Danish army. Over the years, many skeletons have been discovered, said to date from this battle. However, they appear to date from the late seventh century. Otford has entertained many famous names. There was a palace here by 1150, and King Edward I was entertained there by Archbishop Winchelsea. Kings Henry VII and VIII were visitors, and Henry VIII once camped here with his army of five thousand men.

OTFORD UNDER THE HILL. 2772.

Otford, Kent

Little appears to have changed in Otford between these two photographs. Part of the cottages on the left used to belong to the village blacksmith. His old forge, which has long since been demolished, used to be just to the left, out of shot. The building is oak framed and dates from the seventeenth century. Today it is used as a restaurant. Several buildings further up the road, towards the village pond, is the old village workhouse, which had been converted into three residential buildings by 1835. All the residential buildings seen on the left in the old photograph have now been turned into commercial premises. Elsewhere in the village, there has been much residential development. In the 1930s William B. Collier, a local real estate developer, purchased land adjacent to the palace ruins for a development known as the palace estate. The development took place on Pilgrims Road, Parkhill and Beech Lees Road, and included many different styles of house.

Long Barn is in fact two separate buildings joined to make extra living accommodation. The cottage dates from the fifteenth century and was built on this site. The barn, to the right was constructed to the south of the village of Weald some distance from the cottage on a farm track. It remained this way until September 1915 when Vita Sackville-West from Knole and her husband, Harold Nicolson, purchased both the cottage and the barn. At this time, the barn was being used as a garage. Within two months of the purchase, the barn had been carefully dismantled. It was then re-assembled next to the cottage and at the same time converted into living accommodation. It has been said that the cottage was the birthplace of the printer William Caxton,

but Long Barn has become more well known through the autobiography of Vita Sackville-West. For a couple of years, between 1936–38, it was also the home to Charles Lindbergh, the aviator, and his wife Ann.

LONG BARN, WEALD.

H J Han,
Post Office, Weald

Fawke Wood is situated on the southern outskirts of Sevenoaks. It was built on land purchased in 1901 from the Earl of Derby, the owner of Knole at the time, by Mary Blagden. The house was built later that decade. The garden was designed by the famous horticulturist Gertrude Jekyll in 1919. Her association with the architect Sir Edwin Lutyens led to over three hundred gardens being designed by her for his buildings. The house has also been owned by Mr R.V. Toynbee, a name with much heritage in the town. Since the old photograph, the house has been remodelled and extended into two properties, Fawke Wood and Farthings. This is likely to have occurred in 1969 when the property was purchased by Broadland Properties Ltd.